CYSTIC FIBROSIS

CYSTIC FIBROSIS

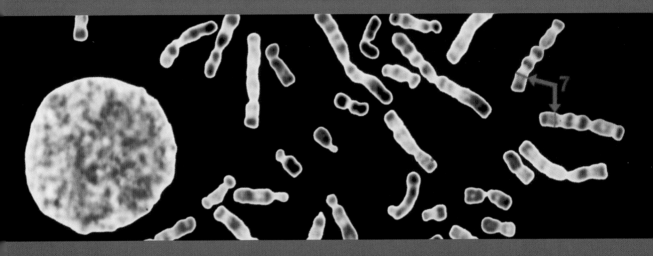

Ruth Bjorklund

Marshall Cavendish
Benchmark
New York

With thanks to Dr. Scott Donaldson, assistant professor of medicine, University of North Carolina at Chapel Hill, for his expert review of the manuscript.

Marshall Cavendish Benchmark
99 White Plains Road
Tarrytown, New York 10591-5502
www.marshallcavendish.us

This book is not intended for use as a substitute for advice, consultation, or treatment by a licensed medical practitioner. The reader is advised that no action of a medical nature should be taken without consultation with a licensed medical practitioner, including action that may seem to be indicated by the contents of this work, since individual circumstances vary and medical standards, knowledge, and practices change with time. The publisher, author, and medical consultants disclaim all liability and cannot be held responsible for any problems that may arise from the use of this book.

Library of Congress Cataloging-in-Publication Data

Bjorklund, Ruth.
Cystic fibrosis / by Ruth Bjorklund.
p. cm. — (Health alert)
Includes index.
Summary: "Provides comprehensive information on the causes, treatment, and history of cystic fibrosis"—Provided by publisher.
ISBN 978-0-7614-2912-8
1. Cystic fibrosis—Juvenile literature. I. Title.
RC858.C95B56 2009
616.3'7—dc22

2007046674

Front cover: Chest x-ray showing cystic fibrosis in the lungs
Title page: Human chromosomes showing gene 7, which determines the occurrence of cystic fibrosis
Photo Research by Candlepants Incorporated
Cover Photo: Simon Fraser / Photo Researchers Inc.

The photographs in this book are used by permission and through the courtesy of:
PhotoTakeUSA.com: Jean Claude Revy/ ISM, 3, 13. *Photo Researchers Inc.*: Phanie, 5, 27, 16; Vero/Carlo, 21; Geoff Tompkinson, 28; Michelle Del Guercio, 41; Mauro Fermariello, 44; Simon Fraser/RVI, Newcastle upon Tyne, 52. *Corbis*: Karen Kasmauski, 8; Mike Kepka/San Francisco Chronicle, 10; Azzara Steve/Sygma, 14; Visuals Unlimited, 17, 23; Bettmann, 32; LWA-Dann Tardif/zefa, 35; Annie Griffiths Belt, 42; Mediscan, 43; LWA-Dann Tardif, 55; Heide Benser/zefa, 56. *Getty Images*: 3D4Medical.com, 19. *Alamy Images*: AGStockUSA, Inc., 25; Tim Hill , 48; Profimedia International s.r.o, 51. *Sciencefaction.net*: CMSP, 36. *AP Images*: Haggerty Family via the Homer Tribune, 38; Marcus Marter/South Bend Tribune, 46; Jim McKnight, 33.

Editor: Joy Bean
Publisher: Michelle Bisson
Art Director: Anahid Hamparian

Printed in Malaysia
6 5 4 3 2 1

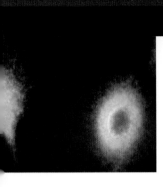

CONTENTS

1

DALE'S STORY

Young people with cystic fibrosis are no strangers to a hospital stay. Among themselves, they jokingly say they are off to "Club Med." Dale is one such person.

Dale was **diagnosed** with cystic fibrosis when he was four months old. His mother tells him that during his first few months he was an especially hungry baby. His diapers were particularly messy and pretty stinky. He tasted salty when she kissed him. His doctor was concerned when Dale was not growing as he should have been. After a few tests, one of which is called a **sweat test**, the doctor discovered that Dale had cystic fibrosis. Cystic fibrosis is an inherited disease for which there is no cure. The disease mostly affects the lungs and digestive system by blocking organ passageways with a thick mucus, making breathing and digesting food difficult.

Dale's parents were shocked when they heard the diagnosis. All they knew about cystic fibrosis was that people who had the disease tended to be very thin and did not live very long.

But doctors and nurses assured Dale's parents that this did not have to be true today. Many people with the disease can live into their thirties or forties. The doctors told Dale's parents that there are even people with cystic fibrosis that have become grandparents! "We found it early, so we can begin treatment early," the doctor told Dale's parents.

So treatments for Dale began when he was four months old. Every day Dale inhaled a steamy medicine through a machine called a **nebulizer**. At least twice a day, one of Dale's parents cupped his or her hands and thumped on his back and chest for a half hour or so, like someone doing martial arts. "Kee-YAH," his father would often say. The thumping helped Dale spit up the mucus that was clogging his lungs. In his bedroom was the nebulizer, which mixed medicine and salt water and made a mist for him to breathe in. He could always breathe more easily after treatments.

When Dale got older, he argued with his mother about his daily treatments. He wanted to get up and get going in the morning. But every day he woke up coughing. Once he started school, he did not want to come home afterward for treatments, either. But Dale knew he needed the treatments to grow and stay healthy. Other than squabbling about taking medicine and having treatments two or three times a day, Dale was in most other ways an ordinary boy. He played soccer and Little League baseball. He had friends and went to school. He grumbled about having to do homework.

In order to stay healthy, a person with cystic fibrosis must have daily medical treatments.

Some things about his disease did set him apart, however. Dale coughed a lot, sometimes until he gagged and threw up mucus he had swallowed. But that was good for him, to get the mucus in his lungs out. Though it sounded painful, Dale told his classmates that he always felt better afterward. Before lunch every day, he visited the health room to take pills that helped him digest his food. Then he was able to eat lunch with his friends in the cafeteria. Some days, he would buy a school lunch *and* eat a sack lunch. His friends were always amazed at how much he could eat and still stay so thin. It was because of the disease.

Winter was a difficult time for Dale. Kids in school had colds and the germs were everywhere. When Dale caught a cold, it was more than a runny nose. The cold and flu germs went into his lungs and serious infections grew.

One year, Dale's cold would not go away. He felt starved for air. When he visited his doctor, she tested his **sputum**, or spit, and how much air his lungs could hold. When too many bacteria showed up in Dale's sputum, he was off to "Club Med." Dale needed **antibiotics**, or medicines that would fight the bacteria growing in his lungs. These drugs were powerful and had to be taken by **IV** directly into his blood.

After he registered at the hospital admissions desk, was weighed, and was shown his room, Dale's caregivers arrived. A technician took his vital signs—his temperature, blood pressure, and the measure of oxygen in his blood. A nurse placed an IV needle into a vein in his arm.

Then his day began. His RT, or respiratory therapist, gave him treatments to open his airways and loosen the mucus in his lungs. Dale had to take two kinds of antibiotics: one taken orally and one intravenously. Some of the medicine tasted bad and some of the machines put a lot of pressure on his sore lungs. Liquid antibiotics were placed in a bag hung on an IV pole. The IV pumped a slow drip of medicine into his veins. After a half hour or so, an alarm alerted the RT that the medicine had finished. The nurse capped off the IV needle in

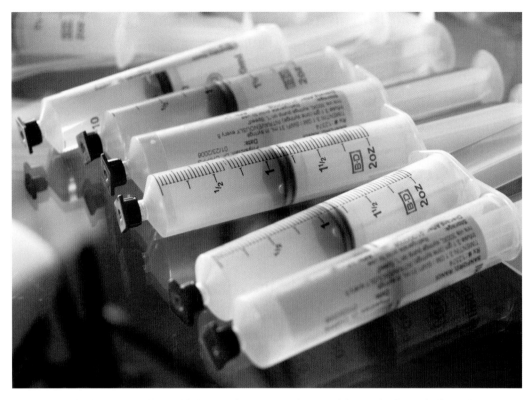

These vials hold antibiotics, which are given to patients with cystic fibrosis in order to keep infections from attacking the body.

his arm until it was needed again. Then Dale could move around for a bit. Moving around was not so easy the first few days, however. His lungs ached and his muscles were weak. But after a few days of treatment, Dale felt better. He amused himself with video games and rode a stationary bike for exercise. Though he grew somewhat bored during his stay, he was rarely alone. In the evening, there were visitors, and during the day someone was always coming into his room to take a blood sample, start the IV, take his vital signs, or wheel him away for a chest X-ray or a lung function test.

Being in the hospital was not fun. Dale missed school and his friends. He could not visit with other patients in the ward because people with cystic fibrosis who have lung infections can infect each other. He hated being sick. He hoped his doctor would let him go back to school. But his mother told him the doctor would probably say he had to stay home for the rest of the year. If he had a tutor, Dale's mother said, he could keep up with schoolwork and stay in the same grade as his friends. Dale knew that in the years to come, there would be good days and bad days.

2

WHAT IS CYSTIC FIBROSIS?

Cystic fibrosis (CF) is a disease caused by a **mutated gene.** A gene is a tiny chemical unit found in living organisms that passes characteristics (such as blood type, height, or hair color) from parents to children. A mutated gene is one that has been damaged or changed and may cause one of the body's proteins to develop abnormally. A person with cystic fibrosis inherits two mutated CF genes, one from each parent.

Every person who has cystic fibrosis is born with the disease. The disease cannot be developed after birth, nor is it contagious (meaning that it cannot be passed from one person to another). Some people with the disease show **symptoms** soon after birth or have symptoms detected before they are born, while others are not aware that they have cystic fibrosis until they are in their teens or have reached adulthood. But most people with the disease are diagnosed by the age of three. In the United States, more than 30,000 children and

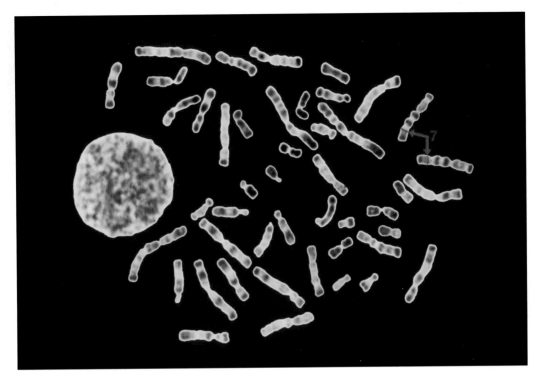

Gene 7 is the gene which mutates in the body and causes cystic fibrosis.

adults have the disease, and nearly 12 million people carry the mutated cystic fibrosis gene.

Scientists have not yet discovered a cure for cystic fibrosis. It is the second most common life-shortening genetic disease in America today, behind only sickle cell anemia. Caucasians of northern European ancestry are most affected, but cystic fibrosis affects other groups as well. Worldwide, there are approximately 70,000 people who have the disease. New treatments and therapies have developed rapidly in recent years, however. In the 1960s, a person with cystic fibrosis

Finding Money for Research

Boomer Esiason and his family pose for a photo at the movie premiere of Rocky and Bullwinkle in New York City. Boomer's son, Gunnar, has cystic fibrosis.

In 1965, a woman named Mary Weiss, who had three sons with cystic fibrosis, was volunteering for the Cystic Fibrosis Foundation. Her job was to telephone civic groups in her town—social clubs, business groups, churches, to raise money for research. One of her young sons heard her on the phone. He told her that he knew what she was calling people about. This surprised Mrs. Weiss because she had not told her young children yet that they had cystic fibrosis. She asked her son what he meant, and he replied, "Sixty-five roses." This sweetly innocent remark charmed the mother and she told the Foundation about it. Since then, the term "65 Roses" has been used by the Foundation to name many fund-raising events. There are 65 Roses golf tournaments, 65 Roses galas and balls, 65 Roses bike races, 65 Roses sports auctions. Many pro sports teams sponsor 65 Roses events, since sports and exercise are so important to staying healthy for many with cystic fibrosis.

Boomer Esiason, a former NFL quarterback, leads another cystic fibrosis fund-raising organization—the Boomer Esiason Foundation. His son was diagnosed with the disease in 1993. Since then, his foundation has raised money for research, scholarships, and financial help for families with large medical bills due to cystic fibrosis.

One man who raises money for Boomer's foundation is Scott Johnson, a thirty-five-year-old athlete with CF. He competes for Team Boomer in Ironman competitions—by swimming 2.4 miles (3.8 kilometers), biking 112 miles (180 km), and running 26.2 miles (42 km). He tells others, "Maintain a positive outlook, don't give up, and keep exercising."

rarely lived to be twelve years old. Now, the median life span of a person with CF has increased to about thirty-seven years in the United States—double what it was just twenty years ago. Today, many people with cystic fibrosis are healthier and more active than in years past.

HOW DOES CF AFFECT A PERSON?

People with cystic fibrosis have a variety of symptoms. Some cases of CF are mild, while others are severe. All, however, are treatable, though not curable. Scientists and doctors report that there are more than one thousand ways the CF gene can mutate, and the various mutations could possibly cause the different symptoms. The CF gene, which has the scientific name ABCC7, makes a protein called CFTR (cystic fibrosis transmembrane conductance regulator). The CFTR protein is found in cells called **epithelial** cells which form a lining inside many organs.

In people without cystic fibrosis, the CFTR protein controls a healthy flow of salt and water through epithelial cells. As a result, it keeps mucus on the inside of the body's organs thin and watery. This is important because mucus protects not only the lining of the lungs, but it also protects the lining of the liver and **pancreas** glands, digestive organs, and reproductive systems as well.

A person with cystic fibrosis, however, has a mutated CF gene that cannot make healthy CFTR protein. As a result, salt

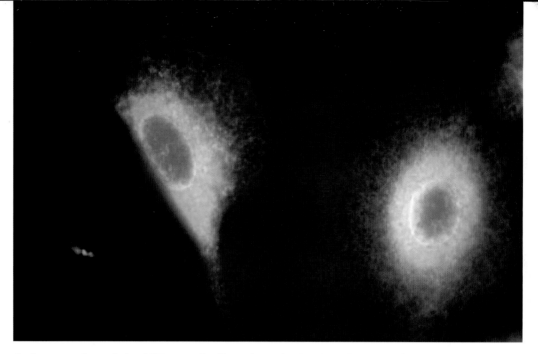

A close-up view of the CFTR protein (in red on the border of the cells), which is made by the cystic fibrosis gene.

does not pass through cells normally. Without the healthy CFTR protein the body needs in order to balance salt and water, people with CF lose too much salt in their sweat and make mucus that is too thick and very sticky. The thick mucus clogs the passageways and linings, and prevents organs from functioning normally.

CYSTIC FIBROSIS AND THE RESPIRATORY SYSTEM

The respiratory system supplies oxygen to the body. Oxygen first enters the body when air is taken in through the nose or mouth and travels down a tube called the trachea. Once it nears the lungs, the trachea splits into two airways called bronchi that enter the right and left lungs. These airways then branch into smaller airways called bronchioles and finally into very small sacs called alveoli. Surrounding the alveoli are tiny blood vessels called capillaries. When oxygen-rich air is breathed in, it makes its way to the alveoli, which inflate and pass the oxygen to the capillaries that deliver oxygen to the bloodstream. In return, the capillaries transfer carbon dioxide from the blood to the alveoli. This waste gas goes back through the airways and is breathed out.

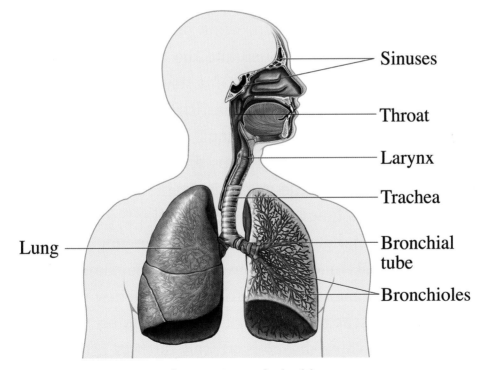

Sinuses

Throat

Larynx

Trachea

Bronchial tube

Bronchioles

Lung

The human respiratory system of a healthy person.

In a person without CF, the healthy mucus keeps the lungs moist and the air flowing smoothly. Mucus also traps any dirt and germs that are inhaled. Tiny hairs in the airways called **cilia** help move the mucus. Their waving motion pushes the mucus and any captured particles up and out of the lungs. The mucus flushes the dirt and germs so that they can be swallowed, sneezed, or coughed out.

For people with cystic fibrosis, however, the CFTR protein in the epithelial cells produces mucus that is thick and gluey. The thick mucus blocks the airways and makes the transfer of oxygen and carbon dioxide difficult. As the airways become blocked, the body lacks oxygen, while poisonous carbon dioxide builds up. With too little oxygen and too much carbon dioxide in the blood, the heart strains itself by pumping harder than it should, trying to get oxygen-rich blood to the body.

As does normal mucus in the lungs, the thick mucus found in a person with cystic fibrosis traps dirt and germs. But because it is too sticky, the mucus is unable to flush the particles out of the lungs. Instead of clearing the airways, it clogs them. Dirt and germs trapped inside the lungs cause serious, life-threatening infections such as pneumonia or bronchitis. Over time, these infections permanently damage the lungs and cause **scar tissue**. Thick mucus clogging the lungs causes other breathing disorders as well, such as asthma, chronic bronchitis, and inflamed sinuses.

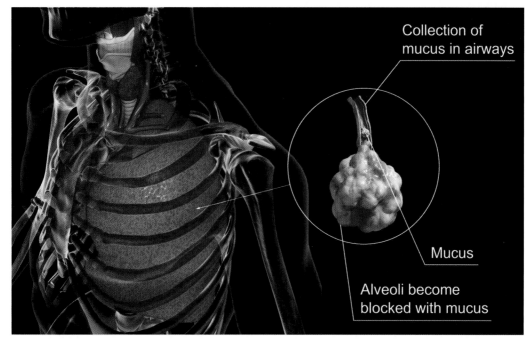

Collection of
mucus in airways

Mucus

Alveoli become
blocked with mucus

This digital image shows how mucus can collect in the airways of a person with cystic fibrosis, making it hard to breathe.

Many people with CF live with lung damage and a lack of sufficient oxygen. After several years, however, they may develop a condition called clubbing. Clubbing is a thickening under the fingernails and sometimes under the toenails which makes the fingers and toes appear club-shaped. Often, clubbed fingers and toes are bluish in color.

THE DIGESTIVE SYSTEM AND CYSTIC FIBROSIS

Digestion is the process that changes food and drink into nutrients that the body can absorb and also use for energy.

The process begins in the mouth where food is chewed. Chewing breaks the food down into smaller pieces. After the food is swallowed, it travels down the esophagus, a tube that connects the mouth to the stomach. In the stomach, powerful proteins called **enzymes** break the food down even more and make it more usable. Then the food passes to the small intestine. There enzymes break down fats, starches, and proteins, and turn them into vitamins and other nutrients needed by the body. Many of the enzymes found in the small intestine come from the pancreas. The pancreas is an organ near the stomach that produces **hormones** and enzymes which are secreted through passageways called **ducts**. After the nutrients are absorbed, the remaining waste moves to the large intestine and is later passed out of the body as **stool** (or feces) through the anus.

Epithelial cells are found in the ducts of the pancreas. Having a mutated CF gene in the lining of these ducts causes mucus to become thick which blocks digestive enzymes from passing into the small intestine. Most people with CF have difficulty digesting their food. They can suffer from painful stomach cramps, **diarrhea**, foul-smelling and oily stools, malnutrition, poor growth, and weight loss. Infants with cystic fibrosis may experience a dangerous condition soon after birth called **meconium ileus** which is a blockage of the intestine caused by thick mucus and stool. The blockage is often removed by surgery.

The pancreas also secretes hormones, which are chemical messengers that control body functions. One of these hormones is insulin, which manages the level of glucose, or sugar, in the blood. When food is digested, it is turned into glucose, the main source of energy for the body. Glucose passes into the blood from the small intestine. Insulin then moves the glucose out of the blood and into the body's cells to nourish them. When the pancreas of someone with cystic fibrosis fills up with mucus, enzymes cannot flow through the ducts. When the enzymes back up, they eat away at the pancreas, causing scarring. Scarring eventually destroys the cells that make insulin. Without insulin, glucose builds up in the blood, causing a form of **diabetes**, a serious disease with symptoms such as excessive thirst, weight loss, frequent urination, extreme hunger, and overall lack of energy.

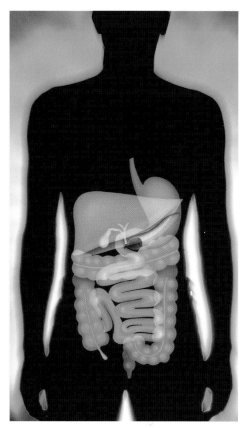

The digestive tract is seen here, with the pancreas highlighted. The pancreas controls hormones, which control body functions.

The liver is another organ in the digestive system that can be affected by the mutated CF gene. The liver plays many important roles. A large artery and a large vein flow into the liver, branching off into smaller vessels. While blood passes through it, the liver removes nutrients to make components for blood cells. It also stores vitamins and minerals and cleans the blood of toxic substances (such as drugs or bacteria). The liver also makes **bile**, a yellowish-green fluid that flows out of the liver. The bile passes through bile ducts into another organ called the gall bladder and also into the small intestine to aid in digesting fats. Because the normal CFTR protein found in the lining of the ducts is missing in someone with cystic fibrosis, the secretions produced here become thickened and the bile ducts become blocked, causing scar tissue in the liver and a buildup of toxic substances. Severe liver damage can cause swelling of the abdomen, yellow skin and eyes, changes in the color of stool and urine, itchy skin, tiredness and confusion, and bleeding in the digestive tract.

CF IN OTHER PARTS OF THE BODY

The largest organ in the body is the skin. The outer layer is made of special epithelial cells. Hair and the CFTR protein live within these cells in **sweat glands** that lie beneath the surface of the skin. Sweat glands produce water that the body relies on to maintain temperature. When the body's temperature becomes too warm, the sweat glands produce salt and water that is

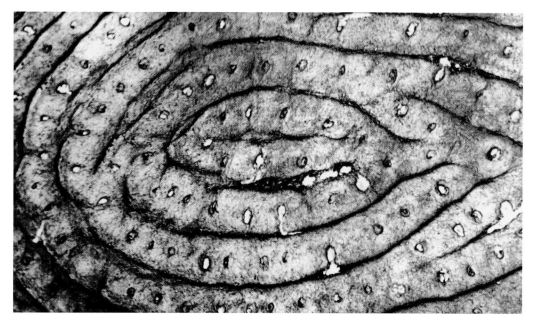

The sweat glands in a human fingerprint are seen here. Body temperature is controlled through the sweat glands, which produce salt and water.

carried to the surface of the skin through sweat ducts. Once on the skin, the water evaporates and cools the body, and the salt is reabsorbed to be used again. People generally produce about two cups of sweat a day, more in warm weather.

In a person with cystic fibrosis, the missing CFTR protein that normally is located in the sweat glands prevents salt from passing through cells normally, so the sweat is extra salty. In hot weather, if too much salt is lost in the sweat, salt levels go below normal in the body, and CF sufferers may experience weakness, fevers, muscle cramps, stomach pain, vomiting, **dehydration**, heatstroke, and exhaustion.

Doctors and scientists marvel at how destructive the mutated CF gene is. It attacks many of the necessary and important systems in the body. It damages the respiratory and digestive systems, as well as the reproductive system. In the reproductive system of males, mucus blocks the tube, called the *vas deferens*, that delivers sperm from the testes to the penis. Most males with CF are sterile, or unable to father children. In females, mucus in the cervix can block the sperm from reaching the egg. However, with good medical care, a healthy woman with CF may be able to bear children.

DIAGNOSING CF

According to the American Lung Association, about one thousand people in the United States are diagnosed with cystic fibrosis each year. Sometimes the diagnosis occurs before a baby is born, but many infants are diagnosed shortly after birth. Approximately 15 to 20 percent of infants with cystic fibrosis are born with *meconium ileus*. Most often, infants with this condition are tested for cystic fibrosis. Many other infants that do not have this condition are diagnosed four to six weeks later when parents and doctors notice that the infant coughs frequently and has not gained weight, even though it is eating enough. This is because the mucus has prevented the enzymes from helping the baby digest food. Still

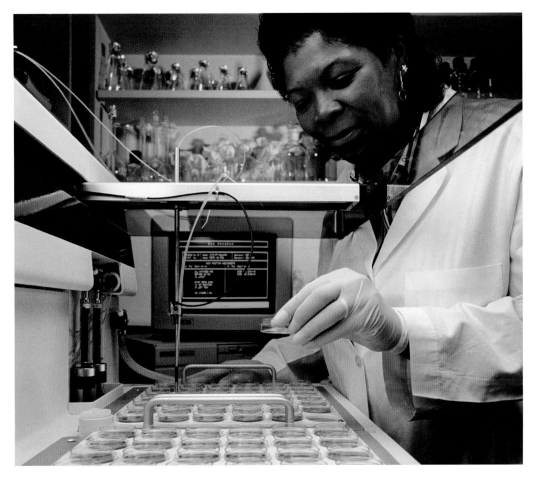

Cystic fibrosis is diagnosed in a laboratory. Here, a scientist performs a chromosome analysis on cells to determine if there are any mutations.

later, some babies and toddlers with cystic fibrosis are diagnosed when parents notice that their children cough too much, gag, vomit, or have frequent oily and foul-smelling bowel movements. To test for cystic fibrosis, doctors often use a very basic test called a sweat test.

Clinical Trials

....

After many years of research developing a drug, scientists must finally test the drug on people to know if the drug is safe and useful. This test is called a clinical drug trial. Trials can last anywhere from weeks to years. In testing the unknown, there are always risks and side effects involved. To protect patients, the U.S. Food and Drug Administration (FDA) has strict rules for clinical trials and must approve a drug's safety before allowing it to be sold in pharmacies. People of all ages with CF are needed to volunteer. Many do, hoping to help find a cure or discover treatments that are less painful and more effective.

The Cystic Fibrosis Foundation and other CF research organizations have worked to convince the FDA to allow more people to participate in clinical trials. There are many promising new drugs ready to be tested and CF groups want volunteers. To find information about clinical drug trials, visit the Web sites of the National Institutes of Health or the Cystic Fibrosis Foundation:

http://clinicaltrials.gov/search/term=cystic+fibrosis

www.cff.org/research/ClinicalResearch/Find/

A sweat test is a simple test which can be done on infants and adults alike. A medical care provider first washes and dries the skin and places gauze pads on either the arm or thigh. One of the gauze pads is soaked in salt water, and the other contains a medication which makes the skin sweat. Electrodes are attached to the pads which, by using a gentle electric current, force the medication into the skin. After a few minutes,

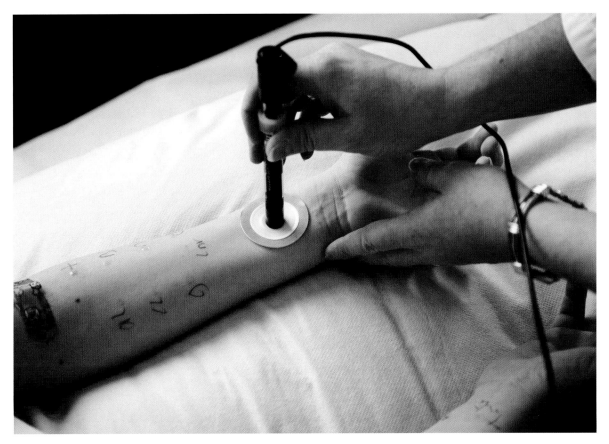

A sweat test is a painless method that detects if a person has cystic fibrosis.

the electrodes and pads are removed. A dry pad or tube is taped on the area for thirty minutes. Then it is removed and sent to a laboratory for testing. The laboratory tests for the amount of salt (the chemicals sodium and chloride) in the sweat. Results take a couple of days. A person with cystic fibrosis will have two to five times more salt in their sweat than a person without the disease.

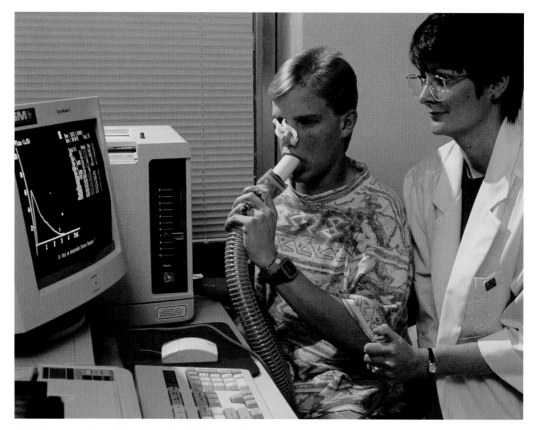

A Pulmonary Function Test (PFT) determines the amount of air that moves in and out of the lungs. A poor result could mean the presence of cystic fibrosis in the body.

If the results are not completely clear, other tests can be done, such as chest X-rays, stool analysis, genetic testing, and **pulmonary** function tests (called PFTs). Pulmonary function tests measure the ability of the lungs to move air in and out. In a stool analysis, a sample of the person's stool is sent to a laboratory where technicians analyze it for enzymes, fats, and other factors that can show problems of the liver or pancreas. A genetic test takes a sample of a person's cells and looks at the genes to find any changes or mutations. But, as there are more than one thousand possible mutations to the CF gene, this is not a test used to initially diagnose whether or not a person has CF. The genetic test is very expensive and not always informative, but it can be the answer for a family that has a history of cystic fibrosis. The test can be done before a baby is born or it can be done on parents who are thinking of having a child and want to know their chances of having a child with CF. Most states are now requiring hospitals to offer genetic testing, or screening, for cystic fibrosis for all newborn babies.

3

THE HISTORY OF CYSTIC FIBROSIS

Cystic fibrosis has likely been affecting humans since the Middle Ages. Recorded in a book titled *German Children's Songs and Games of Switzerland* is a saying, "Woe to that child which when kissed on the forehead tastes salty. He is bewitched and soon must die." In the early 1600s, a Spanish professor of medicine declared that children who taste salty are bewitched. Yet early deaths among children were far more common in times past than they are today, so people then did not suspect that salty skin belonged to a particular disease.

So it was that cystic fibrosis went largely unstudied until the early 1900s. In 1905, a doctor wrote about babies who were born with meconium ileus, coughed a lot, and died young. Six years later, another doctor saw young children ill with both serious lung infections and oily, foul-smelling stools. He believed that possibly they shared a disease and that it might be inherited. Not until the 1930s did scientists and doctors begin to conclude that these symptoms belonged to one disease. A few believed the disease was caused by a lack of vitamin A. In 1938, a doctor named Dorothy Andersen at the Babies' Hospital of New York, wrote a paper describing babies who had died from severe damage to the pancreas as well as lung disease. She named the disease cystic fibrosis of the pancreas. Cystic refers to cysts, which are infected, fluid-filled sacs, and fibrosis is a word that refers to fibers of scar tissue, all of which she found in the pancreases of the deceased children.

In 1944, a doctor in Boston noted that cystic fibrosis was more than a disease of the pancreas. He saw that the lungs and other mucus-producing areas of the body were also affected. He renamed the disease *mucoviscidosis*, which means thick mucus disease. During a heat wave in New York City in 1953, a doctor named Paul di Sant'Agnese saw that young children with cystic fibrosis were much more likely to suffer from heat exhaustion, weakness and dehydration than other children. Along with his colleagues, he developed the sweat test for diagnosing cystic fibrosis, which is still in use today.

The Cystic Fibrosis Foundation was established in 1955 to care for children with the disease and to raise funds for medical research. Dr. di Sant'Agnese received the first grant from the foundation to assist him in researching both treatments and a

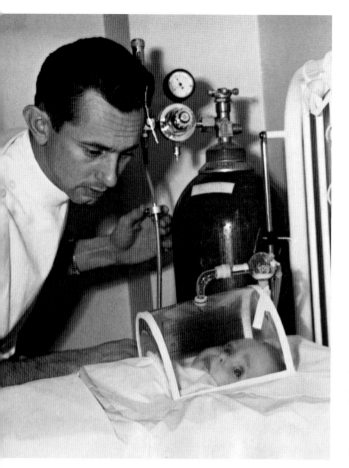

In a photo from 1945, a doctor is seen checking on a seven-month-old cystic fibrosis patient, who is inhaling vaporized penicillin to treat the disease.

cure. Along with Dr. di Sant'Agnese, Dr. Harry Shwachman also received grant money. Dr. Shwachman studied children with cystic fibrosis and found that children with CF who received a diagnosis at a young age—under three months—survived longer and generally led healthier lives. Thus, children who are diagnosed earlier do better because they receive treatment sooner. Dr. Shwachman set the stage for modern treatment today by encouraging doctors and patients to treat lung infections early and to pay close attention to nutritional needs.

The Cystic Fibrosis Foundation began establishing CF care centers, where researchers could study the disease and children with CF could receive expert medical treatment. Having begun with just two facilities in 1961, care centers today number more than one hundred.

LATEST ADVANCES

Cystic fibrosis has proven to be a very complicated disease. Not until 1989 did researchers discover the mutated gene and its defective CFTR protein. This was a huge milestone toward understanding CF. Since then, there have been numerous and rapid advances in treatment. These advances mean more people are living longer, healthier lives. As a matter of fact, today more than 40 percent of people with cystic fibrosis are adults. This means that people with the disease are no longer destined to die young—people with CF are now living longer, thanks to new medications and therapies.

This eighteen-year-old runner has cystic fibrosis. Competing on a track team helps keep her lungs strong.

Medical research into cystic fibrosis takes two main paths—improving the treatment of symptoms and searching for the cause and a cure. For treating symptoms, research has

Who's Who in a Hospital

Many kids with CF are very familiar with their local hospital. They know where the bathrooms are, the playroom, the computer room, the cafeteria, and they know the names of the doctors and nurses. But for those who have not been in the hospital often, it can be a confusing place. Here is a list of some of the people who work in a hospital and the jobs they do.

- **Attending:** The main doctor. He or she will visit once or twice a day and will be the one to decide what medicines to give and when a patient can go home.
- **Fellow:** A doctor next in line to an attending doctor.
- **Resident:** A doctor who has finished medical school and has worked in a hospital but is still in training.
- **Intern:** A first-year resident.
- **Pulmonologist:** A doctor who specializes in diseases of the lungs and respiratory system.
- **Primary Nurse:** The nurse who makes the patient's care plan and is usually the day nurse.
- **Nurse-Practitioner:** A nurse who has completed more years of college than a nurse. He or she may sometimes prescribe medicines.
- **Registered Nurses (RNs) and Licensed Practical Nurses (LPNs):** Nurses that care for patients by running IVs, giving medicines, watching health monitoring machines, and performing other daily care functions.
- **Nurse's Aide:** A helper who takes vital signs, brings food, and changes bed sheets.

A doctor (left) and nurse (right) are two of the people you will see when you spend time in a hospital.

- **Respiratory Therapist (RT):** A specialist who provides airway clearance therapy and gives nebulizer and other inhaled medicines.
- **Physical Therapist (PT):** Specialist who gives chest therapy and who oversees physical activities such as using a treadmill, riding a stationary bicycle, and so on.
- **Lab Tech:** A technician from the laboratory who takes blood, sputum, and other body samples to be studied.
- **Nutritionist:** A specialist who manages a patient's diet.
- **Child Life Specialist:** A person who brings books, art supplies, toys, and games to hospitalized children. May make introductions to other patients, supply DVDs and DVD players, and watch over playroom/ recreation area. May have laptop computers to borrow.

developed new prescription drugs that target lung infections and inflammation, help thin mucus, and address other affected organs such as the pancreas, heart, and liver as well. Lung infections are the most serious concern for people living with CF. As bacteria lodge deep in the lungs, especially the deadly *Pseudomonas aeruginosa* or *Burkholderia cepacia*, the micro-organisms learn to resist antibiotics (medicines that combat bacterial infections), and become harder and harder to kill. Fortunately, today there are many new antibiotics, some created just for CF patients, such as TOBI and *azithromycin*. There are also improved ways of taking the medicines, such as by using a nebulizer or inhaler, or by IV. Researchers have developed drugs, such as DNase, which thins mucus and substances called

Cystic fibrosis patients benefit from taking medicine through new devices, such as this metered dose inhaler.

nucleotides which stimulate cells to secrete salt normally, leading to thinner mucus. They have also found connections in the environment that help with treatments. Researchers noticed that surfers with CF were generally healthier than those with CF who did not surf. They concluded that inhaling a concentrated saltwater solution, called hypertonic saline, could also break up mucus.

Makers of medical equipment have designed special devices such as the **PEP** mask (positive expiratory pressure), the acapella, and the flutter. Each is a device for an airway clearance technique, or ACT. ACTs loosen thick mucus so it can be coughed up. Chest vests are another important type of medical device. They are worn like a vest and thump and vibrate to break up thick mucus in the lungs.

Despite these advances in treating infections and mucus buildup in lungs, there are CF sufferers with lungs that are too damaged to repair. A lung transplant is their final choice for survival. Lung transplants are extremely risky and only about one-third of patients waiting for the operation are able to have surgery. Surgeons must transplant two lungs. Otherwise, the new one would be damaged by the bacteria contained in the old one. The first double-lung transplant for a CF patient was performed in 1983. Since then, surgeons have developed new techniques and new transplant drugs, enabling more people to receive donated lungs. Lung transplants have many side effects and do not cure all aspects of the disease. As an alternative,

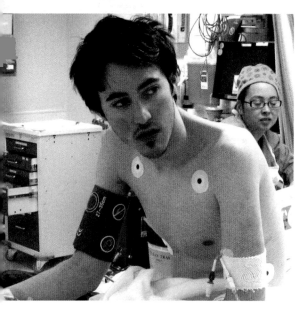

Max Haggerty, a twenty-three-year-old with cystic fibrosis, underwent a double-lung transplant in April of 2007. Today, he is breathing normally for the first time in his life.

surgeons are successfully performing operations that take partial lungs from living donors and transplant them into CF patients.

As Dr. Shwachman saw a half century ago, good nutrition is vital to the health of a person with CF. However, with every meal or snack, people with CF must take enzymes to help digest their food. The enzymes are digestive enzymes taken from animals, usually pigs. People with CF need more protein and energy than others in order to breathe with congested lungs and to fight infections. To grow normally, or to gain or keep up a healthy weight, people with CF who use enzyme therapy must eat and drink 120 to 200 percent more calories than others their age and size. Drug and food companies are developing new high-calorie food supplements that can be made into shakes and smoothies.

As more people with cystic fibrosis live to be adults, many want to be able to have children. Males with CF are often sterile because the sperm cannot pass out of the body to fertilize the egg. But their sperm is healthy. **In vitro** (meaning in a laboratory dish) fertilization makes it possible for a man with CF to father a child and provides a way for other future parents who are at risk of having a child with cystic fibrosis to increase their chances of having a healthy child. In vitro fertilization is a technology that allows doctors to mix sperm and eggs taken from the parents in a laboratory dish. Once the embryo (an organism at the earliest stages of growth) has grown to as few as eight cells, doctors can test for the mutated gene. If there is no mutation of the CF gene, the healthy embryo can be implanted into the mother.

GENE THERAPY

Since 1989, when the defective CF gene was discovered, researchers around the world have dedicated themselves to finding a cure. Using the in vitro technique, scientists have been able to replace a faulty CF gene with a healthy one. To do this, scientists attach the healthy CF gene to a virus that can break through the outer walls of the faulty cell and therefore replace the mutated gene. Clinical trials have shown that this has the potential to work, but in people with CF, the viruses used in the gene therapy treatments can also cause serious infections. Tests on replacing the gene continue while other researchers are developing ways to make the mutated CF protein function more like the normal protein. CF researchers are excited about the rapid progress being made, but know there is much work yet to do. Many believe an answer through gene therapy is near.

4

LIVING WITH CYSTIC FIBROSIS

Unlike some diseases, there is no way to prevent cystic fibrosis completely without testing every person before he or she becomes a parent. And still, at this point in time, most genetic tests are not completely accurate.

Each person has two CF genes. Of those two genes, a person can have one mutated gene without being sick. If a person inherits one healthy CF gene and one defective CF gene, the healthy CF gene will take over. That person will be free of the disease, but will be a carrier of the faulty gene. People can pass either the healthy or the defective gene on to their children. If a person who is a carrier has a child with another carrier, then the chance that their child will have cystic fibrosis is one in four. There is also a one-in-four chance that they will have a healthy child with two normal CF genes. There is a 50 percent chance that the child will be healthy, but be a carrier like the parents. People who have a family history of cystic fibrosis, or suspect that they might be a carrier, often decide to seek

A pregnant couple undergoes genetic counseling in order to understand if they may be carriers of the cystic fibrosis gene.

genetic counseling. Genetic counselors are health care professionals who talk to people who want to have children about their family's medical history. Counselors may advise their patients to have special genetic tests done. If the future parents decide to be tested, the person with the greatest family history of carrying the defective gene will be tested first. As there are numerous ways the gene can mutate, the tests must be very thorough, sometimes testing the person's family as well. If the patient tests positive for the mutated gene, then the other person undergoes the test. If that person does not carry the mutated CF gene, then the couple's children will not have cystic fibrosis, though they could be carriers.

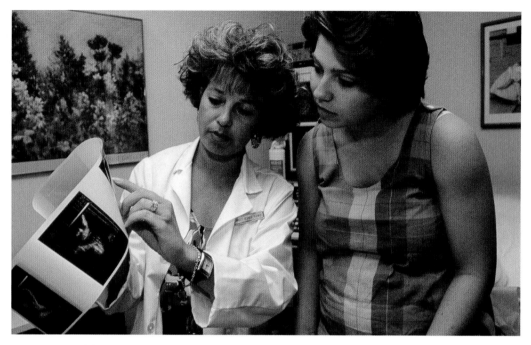

Doctors are able to test unborn babies for cystic fibrosis. Early detection means treatment can begin for an infant soon after birth.

It is possible for a baby to be tested before it is born. This is highly beneficial, because by knowing a baby has the disease at birth, parents and doctors can begin treatment for the infant right away.

TREATING CF

Cystic fibrosis has many symptoms that call for many treatments. Each person with cystic fibrosis has different needs, and anyone with CF should take the treatments very seriously. Even when people with CF are feeling healthy they must spend time each day managing the disease. As one teen with CF advises,

"CFer's should not ignore the fact that while they may be healthy, they are still very delicate."

For most people with cystic fibrosis, lung damage is a serious concern. To keep lungs as healthy as possible for as long as possible, treatment should begin just after diagnosis. When first diagnosed with CF, the patients should visit a cystic fibrosis care center. There, they will receive expert health care and have a treatment plan designed just for them. A pulmonary or respiratory therapist (a technician trained to

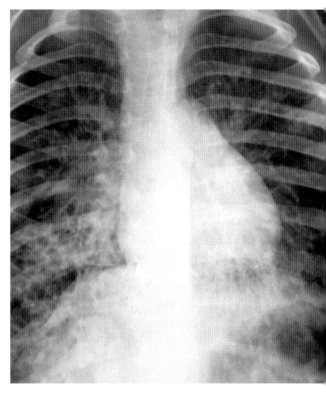

This photo shows a chest x-ray of a person with cystic fibrosis. Sticky mucus clogs up the lungs.

work with people that have lung or respiratory diseases) will show patients and their families airway clearance therapies and how to use and take care of medical equipment. A pulmonologist, a doctor who specializes in cystic fibrosis and lung disease, may prescribe mucus-thinning drugs, medicines to reduce inflammation, or antibiotics to fight infections.

Daily therapy for the lungs can take one to two hours twice or more times each day. Every morning and every night and sometimes at other times during the day, a CF sufferer must practice his or her airway clearance therapy. These therapies break up mucus so that it can be coughed out. The most basic airway clearance therapy is coughing. But coughing does not release all the mucus in the lungs and it can make a person gag, vomit, or feel out of breath. A more effective way of coughing is called huffing. When a person huffs, he or she breathes in and then exhales, making a *huff* sound.

One of the first airway clearance techniques, called chest physical therapy or physiotherapy, is still often used, especially on infants and younger children. To do this form of therapy, the person with CF lies with head down and legs up on pillows or on a special tilting therapy table. A parent, sibling, or other trained caregiver stands over the person and with a cupped

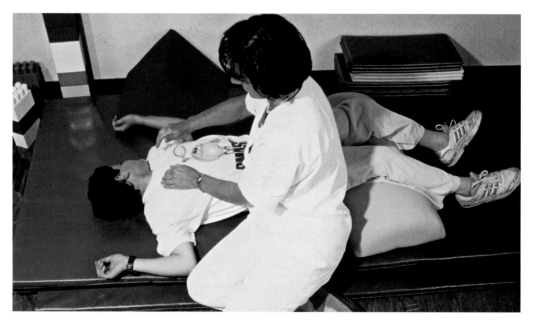

A physiotherapist uses the percussion treatment to loosen mucus in a patient with cystic fibrosis.

hand pounds a section of the chest to loosen the mucus. When the mucus drains downward, the person sits up and coughs the mucus into a cup. Then he or she lies back down in another position and the caregiver thumps on another part of the chest. This is repeated several times each therapy session.

As children get older, they often want to handle more of their therapy themselves. In order to clear their own airways, they can use special airway clearance devices. Some of the devices force air into the lungs to expand the airways and push the mucus forward. Others require the user to exhale into a pipelike device such as the flutter or acapella. Inside the flutter, a steel ball vibrates when the user blows into the mouthpiece. The acapella uses magnets that vibrate. The vibrations travel back to the lungs and help move the mucus. This therapy is part of a group of therapies called PEP, or positive expiratory pressure. By exhaling into these devices, the air pressure in the lungs changes, opening airways and breaking up the mucus. There are also other mechanical devices that replace a care-giver's chest thumping. One, called an IPV (intrapulmonary percussive ventilator), uses jets of air, another device is a vest worn around the chest that vibrates to loosen mucus.

People with cystic fibrosis take many medicines along with airway clearance therapies. **Bronchodilators** are medicines that widen the airways, which may relieve shortness of breath and help clear secretions. Anti-inflammatory medicines such as **corticosteroids** or ibuprofen shrink inflamed and swollen lung tissue, and **mucolyctics**, such as DNase, thin mucus. Many take these medicines with a nebulizer. Liquid medicine is mixed in the nebulizer cup with saline (salt water). A tube is then attached to a machine that blows air into the cup, turning the medicine into a fine mist. The user wears a mask or puts the mouthpiece on and breathes in the mist. The nebulizer has an air compressor attached to it, so it is a large piece of equipment. Some people opt to take only a saline solution through their nebulizer to help cough and break up mucus. In addition, many people with CF carry an emergency handheld inhaler filled

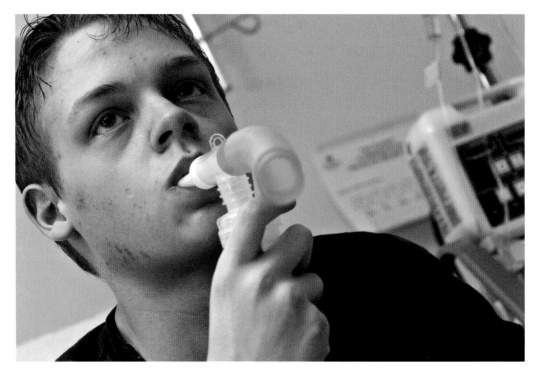

In order to shrink inflamed lung tissue, this cystic fibrosis patient takes medicine from a nebulizer.

with a bronchodilator medicine such as albuterol. When feeling short of breath, they can inhale the drug to open their airways. Others whose lungs are severely damaged may need to carry a portable oxygen tank to maintain their oxygen levels. Some people with CF who cough and wheeze and have trouble sleeping through the night may keep an oxygen tank by their bed and breathe oxygen through a tube as they sleep. There are also smaller, more portable ways of breathing in medicines, such as an MDI (metered dose inhaler) or a powder inhaler. Inhaling medicines is a quicker way of getting medicines to the lungs than swallowing pills and waiting for the pills to go through the digestive system.

Treating the digestive system is often another necessary part of the daily routine. People with CF do not efficiently process the food they eat, especially fats and vitamins, so they need help getting enough energy and nutrients. With each snack or meal, most people with CF must take pancreatic enzymes to help digest their food. Usually taken as a pill or powder, the enzymes are released into the small intestine so that they can break down food to be absorbed into the blood. One blogger on the Internet with CF says that the enzyme pills "save my life every day."

Treatments for cystic fibrosis change as a person ages, so it is important to have a diet plan put together by a nutritionist. Nearly all people with cystic fibrosis should eat a balanced, high-calorie, high-fat, and high-protein diet. As one mother

People with cystic fibrosis need to eat more food than those who are healthy. Milkshakes and other foods high in calories are needed in order to keep the body strong.

says, "Everything they tell you not to eat, my child should eat!" Though this is not entirely true, young people's bodies are growing and children with CF need extra calories to keep their weight up and their bodies healthy and strong enough to fight infections. Most young people with CF are encouraged to double up on foods such as cheese, salt, nuts, ice cream, yogurt, milk shakes, power bars, peanut butter, whole grain breads, pasta, and meats. They should also be sure to have healthy daily servings of fruits and vegetables. Even when eating right, many people with CF must take vitamins every day, especially vitamins A, D, E, and K, otherwise known as ADEKs. Many people with CF do not like the taste of ADEKs, however, so some pharmacies can mix a flavoring into the vitamins. People with CF must also take a daily dose of minerals such as calcium, iron, zinc, and sodium chloride (the salt that CF sufferers lose when they sweat).

Despite the efforts of people with cystic fibrosis and their families to follow the treatment plans, there are times when a visit to the hospital or cystic fibrosis care center is necessary. Common cold and flu viruses are everywhere. There are vaccines for many of them, but not for all. "A normal, healthy person probably gets RSV three times a year and barely realizes it," says Maureen Koval, a pediatrician on Bainbridge Island, Washington. RSV (respiratory syncytial virus) is a virus that causes a common cold and is very contagious, meaning that it spreads easily. "Most children just get a runny nose and the sniffles, but kids with CF can get really sick," the doctor explains. "They are developing a vaccine for RSV but it is the HiB vaccine that has radically changed the outcome for many kids with CF. *Haemophilus influenzae,* or HiB, is a common pathogen, but it can be fatal for a kid with a weak immune system." Doctors recommend that people with cystic fibrosis pay special attention to keeping current with their vaccines. They should get them regularly and be sure to get booster shots when needed.

"It is infection you worry about," says a school nurse. "Winter is the worst." In winter, cold and flu viruses spread easily among students in school. Normally healthy students may miss a few days of school, but students with cystic fibrosis may develop serious lung infections that could require hospital-ization for weeks. Often, the infection is hard to treat with antibiotics, and the student with CF may have to stay away from school until the cold and flu season is over, or longer. "Sometimes I have to tell my patients that they just have to

French Toast Twist

....

Most children with CF should eat high-calorie, high-fat, high-protein foods. This means adding extra ingredients to meals. Here is one easy recipe:

Ingredients
- 2 slices whole grain bread
- 2 tablespoons peanut butter
- 1 tablespoon jelly
- 1 egg
- 2 tablespoons heavy cream
- 2 tablespoons butter
- syrup, extra jam, or powdered sugar

Utensils
- 1 frying pan
- 1 mixing bowl
- 1 spatula
- 1 butter knife
- 1 fork or whisk
- a stove (Be sure there is an adult helping)

Directions:
1. Using the butter knife, spread peanut butter on one slice of bread and jam on the other.
2. Put them together to make a sandwich.
3. In the mixing bowl, add the egg and the cream.
4. Stir with the whisk or fork. Put the frying pan on the stove and set the burner to medium heat.
5. Melt the butter in the pan.
6. Once melted, dip the sandwich into the egg and cream mixture.

7. Place it in the frying pan. Cook until lightly browned, then, using the spatula, flip the sandwich and brown the other side.

8. Remove from pan and serve.

9. Pour syrup, sprinkle powdered sugar, or spread the extra jam on top. Enjoy with a glass of whole milk. (This is approximately 750 calories).

Find other recipes at:

www.kidshealth.org/kid/recipes/cf_recipes/about_cf_recipes.html

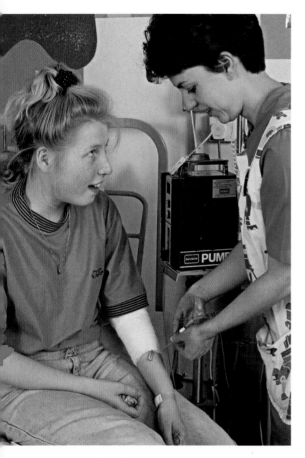

Because their immune systems are challenged, people with cystic fibrosis who catch colds can end up in the hospital.

stay home for the year and see what happens. I know they will miss seeing their friends," says Dr. Koval. "But I say that they can try again next year. I tell them they will get bigger, and their lungs will get bigger."

Unfortunately, there are not vaccines for many of the bacteria and viruses that can cause serious infections in people with cystic fibrosis. Some of these bacteria, such as *Pseudomonas aeruginosa* and *Burkholderia cepacia*, are rarely a problem for people without CF, but for people with CF, the germs collect in their mucus-filled lungs and cause painful inflammation and scarring. The bacteria are very hard to treat with antibiotics and remain deep in the lungs. It is usually these serious infections that bring about what is called end-stage cystic fibrosis. Most people who die of this disease do so because their lungs have become so inflamed and scarred that they are unable to breathe well enough to sustain life. When the lungs fail, the

A 504 Plan

....

In 1973, a law was passed that granted equal opportunities to Americans with disabilities. Section 504 of that law allows children with health needs, such as those with CF, extra accommodations while attending school. Each student's accommodations are put into a plan called a 504 Plan. Once a year, teachers, therapists, parents, and the student have a meeting to decide what should be in the student's plan. Here are some samples of items found in 504 Plans:

- Extra set of books to use at home.
- Permission to sit out some physical education classes.
- Extra snacks and drinks allowed during class time.
- Water bottle allowed on desk.
- Permission to leave classroom to use the bathroom without asking.
- Permission to use bathroom in health room, if privacy is needed.
- Teachers e-mail assignments so students can work from home or hospital.
- School provides a tutor when student misses too much school.
- Assignments are relaxed during periods when student is hospitalized or feeling unwell.
- Treatments, including nebulizer, IVs, or tube feedings are allowed and done in the health room with a school nurse.
- Student, if able to on his or her own, is allowed to take enzyme medications at lunchtime, rather than having to take them before lunch in the health room. (Enzymes should be taken just before eating.)
- Student is able to carry an inhaler.
- Student is allowed to use elevator.

person with cystic fibrosis and his or her family must make emotionally difficult choices. Most want the person to suffer as little pain as possible. Hospitals provide the greatest amount of pain medication and life support. Yet, others may prefer that death come in a hospice or at home, where loved ones can gather in a comfortable or familiar setting to say good-bye and celebrate a life courageously lived.

COPING WITH CF

People with cystic fibrosis often remind others that they are not their disease, their disease is something that they have. It is part of their life's challenge, but it is not what their life is about.

People with cystic fibrosis want to enjoy their friends and family, attend school, participate in fun activities and take pleasure in life. Like other people, they have everyday tasks to perform. Besides brushing their teeth or making their bed in the morning, people with cystic fibrosis also use their nebulizers to take medicines, do their physiotherapy or PEP regimen, or wear their chest vest and swallow a handful of pills at breakfast.

Throughout the course of the day, people with cystic fibrosis must be sure to eat plenty of high-calorie foods and take enzyme tablets along with them. They should exercise as much as possible—play soccer, tennis, cycle, swim, or play whatever sport they enjoy. Exercise breaks up mucus in the lungs, opens airways, and makes lungs stronger. Those with CF who do not or cannot play a sport should try to make walking, going to a fitness center, or doing yoga part of their lifestyle, if they are able. They should also be sure to drink plenty of water and not be afraid to carry tissues and cough into them if necessary.

Some children may not want to tell their friends at school about their disease. They may worry that others will think they are different or that they carry dangerous germs. Ideally though, it is important to know as much as possible about the disease and be comfortable telling others. Teachers and school nurses should be informed that people with cystic fibrosis must have extra fluids and snacks, take vitamins and enzyme pills, and use the

Exercise is an important part of keeping healthy. Playing soccer is just one way to make lungs stronger.

bathroom more often. Fellow students should be told that coughing is good for people with CF and that they are not spreading germs. Classroom booklets explaining cystic fibrosis can be found online: www.cysticfibrosis.com/cfri/cfri_class-room.cfm

Keep it Clean

People with cystic fibrosis, their families, and their friends must pay special attention to staying clean and eliminating the spread of germs.

Clean hands top the list. People should wash their hands with soap and warm water after coughing, sneezing, blowing their nose, spitting up mucus, going to the bathroom, before eating or taking medicines, before doing airway clearance therapies, and whenever their hands look dirty. Antiseptic hand gels are a good way to kill germs and clean hands when water and soap are not available. By carrying a small bottle with them, people can clean their hands after touching things in public places such as schools, stores, and elevators, or after shaking hands.

In order to keep germs from spreading, frequent hand-washing is recommended for anyone who is close to someone suffering from cystic fibrosis.

Keeping medical equipment clean is a major necessity. A nebulizer and all its parts must be washed, sterilized, and air-dried after every use. Nebulizers are made by several manufacturers, so it is best to get cleaning instructions from the instruction booklet each provides. Some nebulizer parts can be boiled, microwaved, soaked in alcohol, or run through a dishwasher to be sterilized.

Developing clean habits is the best way to avoid infection in everyone, especially those with cystic fibrosis.

People with CF must pay close attention to how they are feeling physically and emotionally. It is important to speak up and talk to parents, friends, and health care providers whenever they feel their bodies changing. New treatments are being developed all the time, and doctors and therapists may be able to prescribe medicines or therapies that work better. There may also be clinical drug trials to participate in. Sometimes people with CF feel alone and wish they had a friend with CF to talk to. Frequently though, doctors urge people with CF to avoid each other in social groups as there are germs, such as *Burkholderia cepacia*, that can spread too easily among them. In fact, at one time there were summer camps just for kids with cystic fibrosis, but most of them have been closed due to the worry of infection. But talking does help, and at cystic fibrosis care clinics people can ask for pen pals, cystic fibrosis online chat rooms, or e-mail contacts.

Cystic fibrosis is not a disease with a cure. But, it is a disease that has many health experts actively looking for a cure and devoted to developing treatments that improve the quality of life for people with the disease. As treatments improve, people with CF and their families find new ways to meet the challenges and enjoy lives that are meaningful and full of expe-riences. Today, people with CF are feeling healthier and living longer. They also have reason—now more than ever before—to have hope for a world where cystic fibrosis is a disease of the past.

GLOSSARY

antibiotic—A drug used to treat bacterial infections.

bile—A yellowish-green fluid produced in the liver and stored in the gall bladder that passes to the small intestine to help digest and absorb fats.

bronchodilator—Medicine that widens the airways in the lungs.

cilia—Tiny hair-like structures that wave and move particles through fluid.

corticosteroid—Drug that reduces inflammation.

dehydration—The loss of water and salts needed for normal body function.

diabetes—A disease caused by too little insulin in the blood.

diagnose—To identify an illness.

diarrhea—Frequent, excessive, and watery bowel movements.

duct—A passageway in an organ that fluids pass through.

enzyme—A protein in the body that causes chemical reactions.

epithelial—A layer of tissue forming the lining of passageways, ducts, and organs.

gene—The basic biological unit of heredity.

hormone—A chemical messenger in the body that controls organ function.

in vitro—Latin words used by scientists to mean in a laboratory dish.

insulin—A hormone that is secreted by the pancreas and controls the level of glucose in the blood.

IV—An abbreviation for intravenous which is the injection of fluids and medicine into a vein.

meconium ileus—An obstruction of a newborn's intestines caused by abnormally thick meconium (first bowel movement of a newborn).

mucolyctic—Medicine that thins mucus.

mutate—To change from normal.

nebulizer—A medical device that delivers liquid medicine in a mist form.

pancreas—An organ near the stomach that secretes digestive enzymes and hormones such as insulin.

PEP—An acronym for positive expiratory pressure that is an airway clearance technique in which the user blows or huffs against a resistance.

pulmonary—An adjective referring to the lungs.

scar tissue—Dense, fibrous tissue that forms over a wound.

sputum—A substance made of saliva and mucus that is coughed up from the respiratory tract.

stool—Excrement or feces.

sweat glands—Tubelike structures within the skin that secrete a watery substance.

sweat test—A basic test that measures the amounts of sodium and chloride on the skin and helps diagnose cystic fibrosis.

symptom—A sign of a condition or disease.

Organizations

Cystic Fibrosis Foundation
6931 Arlington Road
Bethesda, MD 20814
1-800-FIGHT CF (344-4823)
www.cff.org

Cystic Fibrosis Research Inc.
2672 Bayshore Parkway, Ste. 520
Mountain View, CA 94043
1-650-404-9975
www.cfri.org

Boomer Esiason Foundation
52 Vanderbilt Avenue, 15th Floor
New York, NY 10017
646-344-3765
www.esiason.org

American Lung Association
The American Lung Association®
61 Broadway, 6th Floor

New York, NY 10006
1-800-LUNGUSA (586-4872)
www.lungusa.org

Books

Abramovitz, Melissa. *Cystic Fibrosis*. San Diego: Thomson Gale, 2003.

Napoli, Donna Jo. *Breath*. New York: Atheneum Books for Young Readers, 2003.

Rosaler, Maxine. *Cystic Fibrosis*. New York: The Rosen Publishing Group, 2007.

Web Sites

cysticfibrosis.com for Kids
www.cysticfibrosis.com/cfkids.html

Cystic-L Handbook
http://cystic-l.org/handbook/

Kids Health—Diet & Nutrition
www.kidshealth.org/kid/health_problems/heart/cf_diet.html

Norma Kennedy Plourde, a Canadian nurse with CF
www3.nbnet.nb.ca/normap/CF.htm

National Library of Medicine, MedLine Plus
www.nlm.nih.gov/medlineplus/cysticfibrosis.html

INDEX

Page numbers for illustrations are in **boldface**

ABOUT THE AUTHOR

Ruth Bjorklund lives on Bainbridge Island, a ferry ride away from Seattle, Washington, with her husband, two teenage children, four dogs, and a cat. She has written several books for young people. In writing this one, she has been awed by the bravery, love, support, and devotion expressed by people with cystic fibrosis, their families and friends, caregivers, and all those who strive toward a cure.